D0019421

ISBN 978-1-943521-02-9

Boyack, Connor, author.
Stanfield, Elijah, illustrator.
The Tuttle Twins and the Creature from Jekyll Island / Connor Boyack.

Cover design by Elijah Stanfield
Edited and typeset by Connor Boyack

Printed in the United States

15 14 13 12 11 10 9 8 7

THE TUTTLE TWINS
and the
CREATURE FROM JEKYLL ISLAND

CONNOR BOYACK

Illustrated by Elijah Stanfield

Other books in The Tuttle Twins series:

The Tuttle Twins Learn About the Law
The Tuttle Twins and the Miraculous Pencil
The Tuttle Twins and the Creature from Jekyll Island
The Tuttle Twins and the Food Truck Fiasco
The Tuttle Twins and the Road to Surfdom
The Tuttle Twins and the Golden Rule
The Tuttle Twins and the Search for Atlas
The Tuttle Twins and their Spectacular Show Business

Find them all at TuttleTwins.com

This book is dedicated to
G. Edward Griffin.

His work has helped
weaken the creature's power.

"Suit up, kids—it's time to get some liquid gold from our beehives!" Mr. Tuttle told Ethan and Emily.

One of Mr. Tuttle's favorite hobbies was beekeeping. He and the twins had a deal where he would take care of the bees, and the twins would take care of the honey—the best part!

It had been a productive summer. Their bees
had worked very hard collecting nectar from
all of the flowers and vegetable gardens in the
neighborhood, and turning it all into honey.

Mr. Tuttle opened the first hive and blew some
smoke inside to make sure the bees stayed calm.

Ethan and Emily helped remove the frames full of
honey and carry them to the garage, where they

used an extractor to spin them for a while until all of the honey had come out and dripped down through the filter and into jars.

Emily couldn't resist sticking her finger into the golden waterfall coming out of the extractor. "This tastes amazing, Dad!" she said as Mr. Tuttle smiled.

Even though they were planning to sell a lot of the honey, the Tuttle family made sure to keep several jars for themselves.

By the time they had finished, Grandma and Grandpa Tuttle had arrived. They had come to town for the annual county fair and farmers market—it was everyone's favorite day of the summer.

Emily looked forward to riding the roller coaster. Ethan was excited to eat some cotton candy. They were both excited to sell their jars of honey at their farmers market booth!

Later that day, Grandma and Grandpa Tuttle surprised the twins with a trip to the movies. Ethan had been begging to see the latest superhero movie at the new theater that showed movies in 3-D and had seats that vibrated to make the movie feel more real.

At the movie theater, Grandpa Tuttle was amazed at the price of the tickets. "I paid 50 cents for a movie ticket when I was your age, and now it costs over twenty times that much!" he said.

"Can we get some popcorn?" asked Ethan. "And something to drink?" asked Emily.

"You bet," Grandma Tuttle replied.

The cash register rang up at $10. "My heavens, why does everything cost so much these days?" she asked Grandpa Tuttle.

"This night out cost a little more than we had planned," Grandma whispered to Grandpa as they all settled into their seats. "It's because of that wretched creature from Jekyll Island, that's why!" Grandpa complained a little too loudly.

The twins overheard Grandpa. Emily was about to ask what he meant when Ethan suddenly let out a loud shout. His popcorn launched into the air, spilling onto Emily's lap.

As Emily looked up to see what had startled Ethan, her seat vibrated and she let out a scream of her own. A really mean-looking octopus had suddenly filled the movie screen, and its 3-D tentacles seemed to reach out towards the twins.

It was only a preview for another movie and soon their own movie began—but Ethan and Emily couldn't forget how startled they were.

"Mom, the movie was awesome!" Ethan told her as she tucked him into bed that night. She kissed Ethan goodnight, then left to tuck Emily in.

But Ethan couldn't sleep—he was restless, still seeing that scary octopus from the movie theater in his mind.

He could hear his dad and Grandpa Tuttle talking downstairs in the dining room. Ethan could tell that his grandpa was upset about something. He crept down the stairs to better hear what they were saying.

"I don't know how I'm expected to make this work," said Grandpa. "My income isn't going up, but the cost of everything is *definitely* going up. I've worked hard all my life, and now my savings is being stolen."

Ethan saw his dad shake his head slowly. "The creature from Jekyll Island strikes again... Life would be better if it didn't exist," Mr. Tuttle said.

There it was again! That was the second time Ethan had heard about this creature in just one day. But what was it? Why was a creature taking Grandpa's money?

"Wake up, Emily," whispered Ethan into his sister's ear as he shook her.

"Wha- what is it?" Emily stuttered as she came out of a deep sleep. "What's wrong?"

"Remember how Grandpa complained about a creature from Jekyll Island when we were at the movies?" Ethan said. Emily nodded. "Well, Dad knows about it, too. He just talked about it downstairs. What do you think it is?"

"Well, what have they said about it?" asked Emily after a big yawn. "Grandpa said that the creature is the reason why things cost more than they used to."

"And just now, he was talking about his savings being stolen, and Dad blamed it on the creature," Ethan added. "What kind of creature needs money?"

"Let's worry about it in the morning," replied Emily. "I need to sleep so I have lots of energy for the roller coaster ride."

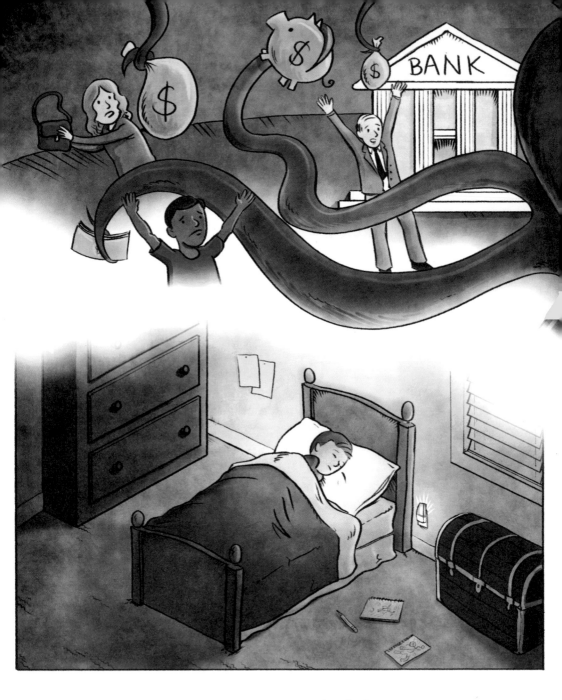

The Tuttle twins both dreamed of the scary octopus that night. Ethan imagined it stealing people's purses and piggy banks.

Emily dreamed of a haunted dungeon on Jekyll Island where a crazy scientist created a monster that grew by eating people's money.

The sun was beaming brightly on the fairgrounds the next morning as the Tuttle family set up their booth and displayed their jars of honey for people to buy.

The fair was packed with people—it reminded Emily of the thousands of bees moving around in their hives, busy at work.

"Hey, neighbors!" said Fred, who was pushing a

wheelbarrow of tomato crates to his booth. Fred was the twins' favorite neighbor and a good friend. "It's a great day to be in business, isn't it?"

"All of those tomatoes came from your garden?" Ethan asked Fred.

"Yep! These and several boxes of other vegetables," Fred replied. "I owe a lot to your bees—they have been doing a great job pollinating my garden!"

Grandpa and Grandma Tuttle set up their chairs in the shade, and settled in to watch Ethan and Emily make some sales. Grandpa began reading the newspaper but was quickly interrupted by Emily.

"Why is a creature taking your money, Grandpa?" she asked curiously.

"Come again?" Grandpa replied.

"Yesterday you were talking about a creature from an island that makes things cost more," Emily explained. "And last night Ethan heard Dad talk about the creature when you said that your savings was being stolen."

"Here we go..." said Grandma quietly, chuckling to herself. "You two better sit down for this," she said to the twins while winking at Grandpa Tuttle.

"Where to begin...?" said Grandpa, rubbing his hands together slowly. "Here's a question: why are you selling honey today?"

Ethan pulled a handful of money from a box and held it up to Grandpa. "Because we want more of this!" he said excitedly.

"And why do you want money?" he asked, looking at Emily. "You can't eat it or play with it."

"So I can ride the roller coaster," she replied, pointing to the sky-high ride across the field. "And get some cotton candy!" Ethan added.

"That money you have is called a *medium of exchange*. It's something that we can use to trade with somebody for things we want—and they can use it to get the things they want," Grandpa explained. "But do you need to use money?" he asked.

"How else would we buy things?" Ethan replied.

"Why don't you try to trade some honey for roller coaster tickets?" Mrs. Tuttle suggested, offering to watch the booth for them.

"Great idea!" said Grandpa. "That's what we call *bartering*. C'mon, let's go ask!"

"Hi there!" Grandpa said to the woman at the ticket counter. "We're wondering if we can barter our honey for a few roller coaster tickets."

"Oooh, I love honey," the woman said. "But I'm sorry—we can't accept it as payment."

"Why didn't that work?" Ethan asked as they walked back to the booth. "She even said that she loved honey! Why wouldn't she trade with us?"

"Well, imagine if everyone tried to barter for tickets," replied Grandpa. "How would a barber take his family on a ride if the roller coaster worker happened to be bald? Or what if a car salesman tried to trade a car for tickets?"

"Wow! A car is probably worth thousands of tickets. There's no way he could use that many," Emily said.

"And even if some of the roller coaster workers wanted a new car, how would they divide it up between themselves?" Grandpa added.

"But when we use money," Grandpa continued, "we don't have to worry about finding somebody else who wants to barter with us. It makes trading a whole lot easier for everyone."

"Okay, I understand that," Emily said. "But what about the creature? What does it have to do with all of that?"

"One of the sneaky things the creature does is make prices go up," Grandpa explained. "Like your Grandma said yesterday, things cost much more today than when we were your age. And it's the creature's fault."

"Imagine if the creature could sneak into the fairgrounds and change the cost of a ticket," he added. "Right now it's $1 for a ticket, but what if the creature made each ticket cost $2?"

Ethan imagined the scary octopus slithering through the fairgrounds late at night, holding markers in its tentacles and writing new prices on everything.

"That would be awful," Ethan said. "We'd have to sell way more honey to earn more money. But I don't get it. How can a creature raise prices? Or steal your money?"

Grandpa waited to answer while the twins sold a jar of honey to a customer for $3.

"The creature isn't an *actual* creature," Grandpa explained. "I just call it that because it kind of acts like one—it does bad things and it usually works in secret so nobody knows what is happening."

"The creature is really a group of powerful people— some from the government who control the laws, and others who are bankers who control money."

"A long time ago after people realized that bartering wasn't working too well, they started to use different things as their money," Grandpa explained.

"Really interesting stuff," interjected Grandma Tuttle, "like sea shells, barley, or rice. Imagine having to carry a pocketful of rice to pay for things at the store!"

"After that, people used gold and silver, right?" asked Emily. "Dad has lots of gold and silver coins he saves."

"Yes, those metals were used as money because they aren't easy to find in the earth—they are very rare. They can also be melted and made into small coins if you needed to spend a smaller amount," Grandpa replied.

"That's why almost everyone accepted gold and silver for thousands of years," he said. "Those coins are a great medium of exchange. But over time, bad people began acting like a sneaky creature, stealing some of the metal."

"There were kings who would secretly shave off the edges of coins to make new ones," Grandpa Tuttle explained, "and turn around and buy food and nice things with the stolen money. The people wondered why they kept having less and the kings and the kings' friends kept getting more. It's because they were cheating by making new money!"

Grandma Tuttle found a quarter and showed it to the twins. "Eventually, people noticed when the coins started to shrink, so they invented new ways to stop those in power from cheating."

"See these ridges?" she asked. "If metal was shaved off the coin, the ridges wouldn't be there, so people would know if some of the metal had been taken."

Ethan had always seen the little bumps on the edges of coins but now he realized what they were for—to tell if the coin had been shaved or not. "Smart idea!" he thought.

"But it didn't stop there!" Grandpa said. "No, powerful people continued to find sneakier ways to make new money and steal from hard-working people, until finally they hatched the trickiest scheme of all time." The story was getting exciting; the twins moved closer to Grandpa Tuttle.

"The year was 1910. A small group of the wealthiest and most powerful bankers in the world, along with a couple of people in the government, held a secret meeting on Jekyll Island, in Georgia, to plan the ultimate bank called the Federal Reserve. This bank—this creature—has one main power, and a very sinister one: *the power to actually make unlimited amounts of new money.*"

"That would be awesome!" shouted Ethan. "If I could make all the money I wanted, I'd be the richest person in the world!"

"That might be good for you," replied Mrs. Tuttle. "But let me teach you why it's a bad thing for everyone else."

"Let's use that cotton candy you want as an example," she said to Ethan. "Imagine there is only one left for sale. I can pay $1 for it, but you created lots of new money, so you can pay $5. Which one of us do you think the vendor will sell that cotton candy to?"

"He'll definitely want the $5 from me." Ethan replied.

"That's right—and when this happens again and again, at all the places your new money is spent, prices start to go up everywhere. The people that get your new money first can buy things before the prices go up, but the people who don't get the new money can't buy as much anymore. Eventually everybody's money is worth less," Mrs. Tuttle added. "This is called *inflation*."

"Well, then I'd have to make even more new money," Ethan said jokingly.

"You're a sneaky one, aren't you?" Grandma Tuttle said playfully.

"That's why I mentioned the creature last night when Grandpa said his savings was being stolen," Mr. Tuttle said.

"Grandpa is retired, and he's not earning new money—so the money he had saved up is becoming worth less every time the Federal Reserve makes new money."

Emily imagined the creature grabbing poor Grandpa and turning him upside down, shaking out his pockets.

"I've seen a video about something like this," Ethan said. "It happened in Germany, right?"

"Oh, yes," Grandpa replied. "After World War I, people would have to bring a wheelbarrow full of money just to pay for a single meal. The creature in that country had created so much new money that it became worth little more than the paper it was printed on."

"Check this out," Mr. Tuttle said, pulling a piece of paper money from his wallet and handing it to the twins. "This was printed in the country of Zimbabwe."

The money said "One Hundred Trillion Dollars." The twins' jaws dropped, and their eyes bulged. "Dad, you're *rich*!" Emily said.

Mr. Tuttle laughed. "Not really—the creature in Zimbabwe printed so much money that it became worthless, and people stopped using it. This sounds like it's a lot of money, but that's the point! There was so much money being made that it couldn't actually buy very many things."

Ethan thought it might be funny to change the booth's sign to read, "Honey: $500 trillion Zimbabwe dollars." He giggled to himself, but decided that most people wouldn't get the joke.

Thankfully, tickets for the roller coaster were still only $1 each and Mrs. Tuttle and Grandma offered to watch the booth while everyone went for a ride. Rather than trying to barter with honey or pay with Zimbabwe dollars, this time Grandpa paid with a $5 bill and purchased a few tickets.

"Making new money isn't even the worst part," Mr. Tuttle stated as they got in line. "The bankers who met at Jekyll Island had friends in the government who helped pass laws that forced everyone to use the new money from the Federal Reserve. When government makes everyone use a certain kind of money for trade, it's called *fiat currency*."

"Because everyone needs a medium of exchange to buy things, having to use the creature's fiat currency gives the creature control over people and can even trick people into buying things they normally wouldn't buy," Mr. Tuttle added.

Emily was doubtful. "How can you trick people into buying something?" she asked.

"The Federal Reserve can make the prices go up and down by adding or taking away how much money there is," Grandpa explained.

"Today you're selling your honey for $3 a jar," he added. "If the creature said it would make the price go down to 50 cents tomorrow, would people buy your honey today, or wait?"

"They would definitely wait to get a better deal tomorrow," Emily answered.

Ethan's eyes lit up as he and his family buckled themselves into the roller coaster. "Or what if the creature was going to make our honey cost $10 tomorrow? Everyone would be rushing to buy it for $3 today before the price went up."

"Exactly riiiiiiiight!" shouted Grandpa as they were flung into the air.

"That sounds like what happened to our neighbors," said Mr. Tuttle at the end of the ride. "A few years ago, the Federal Reserve made the price of homes go down, so they bought several more to rent to others. Then it made prices go up, so people who needed to sell their homes couldn't find any buyers. They ended up losing all the homes they had bought, including their own."

"Now you see why the creature is so dangerous," added Grandpa Tuttle. "A lot of people have suffered around the world because it controls fiat currency and causes inflation."

After they returned to the family's booth, Ethan began doodling on some paper and began drawing a rich man wearing an octopus costume. Suddenly the creature didn't seem so scary anymore. It was just another person—or, really, a group of people trying to control everybody and take their wealth by inflating the money.

Emily grabbed the paper, crumpled it up, and threw it in a trash can. "There, I got rid of the creature!"

"If only it were that easy," chuckled their dad. "Unfortunately there's not much any one person can do about it. The only way to beat the creature is to teach more people about it and get the government to change the laws that require us to use the creature's fiat currency."

"If people could choose what money to use, the creature would lose a lot of its power," concluded Grandpa Tuttle.

"And just like some smart people figured out how to put ridges in coins," added their dad, "smart people today are figuring out how to trade without the creature being able to control them—using things like gold and silver products, garden co-ops, online bartering, and digital currencies such as Bitcoin."

"In a way, the creature acts like you do with the bees," Mrs. Tuttle told the twins. "Powerful people controlling hard workers and taking away their savings... sound familiar?" she asked with a smile.

"Speaking of honey, it looks like we just sold the last of it," Mr. Tuttle said. He paid Ethan and Emily their portion of the money their family earned that day.

Ethan quickly bought some cotton candy from a vendor wandering by their booth. "C'mon, Emily," he beckoned. "Let's go spend our money before the creature makes everything cost more!"

Grandpa Tuttle couldn't stop laughing at Ethan's joke. Mr. Tuttle smiled as his mother put her arm around him. "Those are some very smart kids, son."

The End

The Author

Connor Boyack is president of Libertas Institute, a free market think tank in Utah. He is also president of The Association for Teaching Kids Economics, an organization that provides teachers with educational materials and lesson plans to teach economic ideas to their students in a fun and memorable way. Connor is the author of over a dozen books.

A California native and Brigham Young University graduate, Connor currently resides in Lehi, Utah, with his wife and two children.

The Illustrator

Elijah Stanfield is owner of Red House Motion Imaging, a media production company in Washington.

A longtime student of Austrian economics, history, and the classical liberal philosophy, Elijah has dedicated much of his time and energy to promoting the ideas of free markets and individual liberty. Some of his more notable works include producing eight videos in support of Ron Paul's 2012 presidential candidacy. He currently resides in Richland, Washington, with his wife April and their six children.

Contact us at TuttleTwins.com!

Glossary of Terms

Barter: Exchanging goods or services with another person without using money (or another medium of exchange).

Central Bank: A bank given privileges and authority by a government to control and regulate all other banks and the supply of money in a country.

Economy: The spontaneous interactions of billions of people buying, selling, and exchanging goods and services.

Fiat Currency: Money that derives its value not from any natural characteristics (such as usefulness, desirability, etc.), but from the guarantee of government that it must be accepted and used.

Inflation: An increase of money (such as by printing it), the consequence of which is making the value of existing money go down.

Medium of Exchange: An intermediary (gold, fiat currency, etc.) used in trade to avoid the inconveniences of a pure barter system.

Discussion Questions

1. Why did Grandpa Tuttle's savings become worth less when the "creature" created new money?
2. What would be the disadvantages of a pure barter economy?
3. Why do governments like controlling and creating money?
4. What are the problems with fiat currency—and, more importantly, what money system would be better for the economy?

Don't Forget the Activity Workbook!

Visit **TuttleTwins.com/CreatureWorkbook** to download the PDF and provide your children with all sorts of activities to reinforce the lessons they learned in the book!